# FOLENS IDEAS BANK READING SKILLS IN CONTEXT BOOK 2

Pat Hughes

## Contents



Folens Publishers

# How to use this book

**Ideas Bank** books provide ready to use, practical, photocopiable activity pages for children, **plus** a wealth of ideas for extension and development.

**TEACHER IDEAS PAGE** | **PHOTOCOPIABLE ACTIVITY PAGE**

Clear focus to the activity.

Ideas for introducing the subject.

Suggestions for developing work on the photocopiable pages.

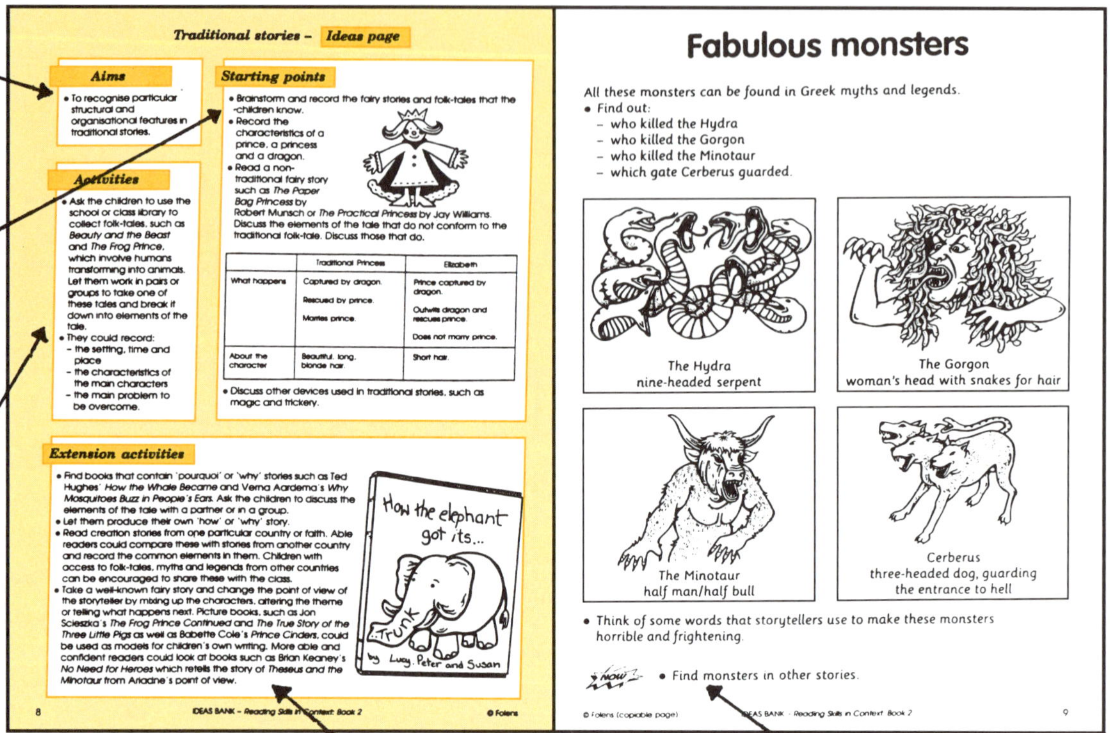


Extension activities suggested to take the work one stage further.

Independent activities for children to work with.




Editor: Andrew Brown. Layout artist: Suzanne Ward. Cover design: In Touch Creative Services.
Illustrations: Susan Hutchison – Graham-Cameron Illustration. Cover image: Sue Woollatt – Graham-Cameron Illustration.





British Library Cataloguing in Publication Data. A catalogue record for this book is available from the British Library.

First published 1996 by Folens Limited, Dunstable and Dublin.

Folens Limited, Albert House, Apex Business Centre, Boscombe Road, Dunstable, LU5 4RL, England.

ISBN 1 85276197–0

Printed in Singapore by Craft Print.

# Introduction

Reading skills are developed within an integrated programme of speaking, listening, reading and writing. The activities suggested in this book cover all these aspects of children's learning and seek to ensure that reading skills are not practised and tested in isolation. Writing is also an act of reading, so when children write or draw to record reading skills, they are reading as well. Children's reading should include texts:

- with challenging subject matter that broadens perspectives and extends thinking
- with more complex narrative structures and sustained ideas
- that include figurative language both in poetry and prose
- with a variety of structural and organisational features.

Literature read should cover a range of modern fiction by significant children's authors; some long-established children's fiction; a range of good quality modern poetry; some classic poetry; texts drawn from a variety of cultures and traditions; myths, legends and traditional stories.

Pupils should read and use a wide range of sources of information, including those not specifically designed for children. The range of non-fiction should include IT-based reference materials, newspapers, encyclopaedias, dictionaries and thesauruses.
(National Curriculum Orders for Reading KS2.)

**Reading skills and fiction texts**
The first eight ideas pages and activity sheets (pages 4–19) provide starting points and practical suggestions for developing reading skills using children's fiction. A look is taken at how to use picture books with older children and suggestions are made for ways in which the children can be encouraged to enjoy pictures and texts at different levels.

The activity pages suggest activities to develop reading skills using different forms of fiction – traditional tales, modern fantasy tales, realistic fiction and historical fiction. Children are encouraged to increase their ability to read fluently with understanding and enjoyment and consider in detail the quality and depth of what they read. The activities explore ways in which they can be helped to respond to what they have read with imagination and to structure this response in terms of plot, characters, ideas and vocabulary.

The two sections on poetry look at rhythm, rhyme, sound and imagery in poems and suggest ways in which children can be introduced to different forms of poetry. The activity sheet 'Rap, rhyme and rhythm' explores ways in which poetry can raise children's awareness of sound effects in poetry to develop their knowledge about language and phonic skills. The 'Story poems' activity sheet looks at how narrative poems can be used to encourage skills in inference and deduction of stories.

As adults we often take advice from friends about what to read. It is important to provide the children with an opportunity to talk about books that they have read and would recommend to others.

**Reading skills and non-fiction texts**
The remaining pages of the book look at identifying and developing reading skills involved with the use of a wide variety of information texts. Ways to develop children's library skills and raise their awareness about the huge variety of information texts that are available in libraries are looked at first. The emphasis moves on to looking at specific skills involved in using dictionaries, thesauruses, encyclopaedias and information books. Support is also given to ways in which children can be taught about different types of reading strategies and how to present them with material that requires the use of these strategies.

An increasing amount of the reading undertaken by children today is via a screen. There is little evidence about how they learn to read from screens, but with the increased use of CD-ROMs in schools, children's ability to make sense of the screen are likely to become even more important.

Finally, a look is taken at the ways in which children can be supported in their use of community texts, such as newspapers, environmental print, travel brochures and junk mail. Today's children live in a world which surrounds them with more print than has ever existed before. Print assaults us in all sizes, shapes, colours and forms. Children need a high degree of sophistication sometimes to even recognise messages that are being sent to them via the printed word. If they are to become skilled in understanding and responding to print they need to become confident readers with the ability to recognise and discard print when they need to, as well as to use their reading to enhance and improve their lives.

# Reading book covers – Ideas page

## Aims

- To use picture book covers to predict content.
- To interpret how pictures and text in picture books have been used.
- To develop skills in using picture books at a more advanced level.

## Activities

- Let the children choose a picture book that they have not read before and predict the story from the front cover. They should read the book and compare their initial prediction with the finished text.
- Give them the activity sheet and read it through with them before asking them to complete the task.
- After the children have completed the sheet, discuss with them why they matched the titles to the pictures and why they wrote the summary that they did. Do they feel that they 'read' the cover pictures correctly?
- Working in pairs with a picture book of their choice, they should read it together and discuss the story. Less able readers could be given books with a very limited vocabulary and/or with a very repetitive text.
- Ask them to either rewrite the story together or write their own story for the pictures. Strips of paper could be fitted over the text and held in place with Blu-tack.

## Starting points

- Make a collection of picture books. These could be books already familiar to the children from when they were younger or books linked to a particular curriculum or PSE theme. Let the children have an opportunity to look at them in detail.
- At a more advanced level, choose one picture book from this collection and read it to the whole class. Discuss the ways in which picture books can be evaluated, for example:

**Content**
- when and where it takes place
- if it is a good story or not
- how the theme/story is developed through the text and pictures
- the age group for which it is written
- if it is really written for children or adults.

**Illustrations**
- if the illustrations help the story.

**Format**
- if the cover shows what the story is going to be about
- if the summary describes the book well.

**Comparisons** (with other picture books)
- if there are other books in the collection by the same author/illustrator
- if there are other books that tell a similar story.

## Extension activities

- Let the children work in pairs or in a small group on a wordless text such as *Window* by Jeannie Baker or *Rainforest* by Helen Coucher. After they have had time to read and discuss the pictures they can make notes about the book and then write a text for it. More able children could be asked to make this suitable for a child of five. They might need to read other picture books suitable for beginning readers to provide a model for their own writing.

- Make a collection of stories by one author, such as Mem Fox, that are illustrated by different people. Ask the children if they think that having different illustrators makes a difference to the mood of the stories.

# What's inside?

- Match the book titles to the cover pictures.
- Choose one and discuss with a friend what the story inside the book might be about.

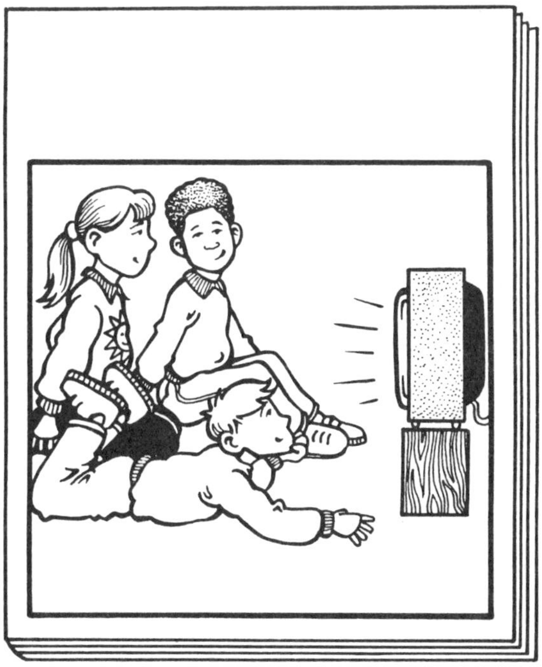

| | | | |
|---|---|---|---|
| Dragon catches cold | Starsearch 2020 | The air-sick duck | Tom's TV gang |

NOW
- Write a summary of the story.

## *Forming opinions – Ideas page*

### Aims

- To share books that they have read with other children.
- To develop the ability to form criteria for choosing fiction for personal reasons.

### Starting points

- Ask the children to bring in a book from home or to find one in the school/class library that they have enjoyed and want to share with others.
- Make a collection of these books and let the children talk about or record details of any books that are the same or have the same author. See if they know other books by the same author.

- Draw up criteria that make a fiction book worth reading, such as:

### Activities

- Ask the children to read a picture book together in groups. Suitable ones might include Maurice Sendak's *Where the Wild Things Are* or John Burningham's *Come Away From the Water, Shirley*. (Alternatively, a Big Book suitable for the age range could be used and carried out as a class activity.)
- Ask the groups to use the activity sheet to record their responses to the book.
- Record and display all the different comments made about the book. Everything said should be recorded without comment to acknowledge that there is no 'right answer'.
- Discuss whether there are any comments that appear in different columns. For example, see if any one child has said that they disliked something and if another has said that the same thing had puzzled them or that they liked it.
- Ask the children what conclusions they can draw from the exercise.

### Extension activities

- In groups of four or in established reading groups, ask the children to read and then discuss a picture book with which they are not familiar. Let them record their findings individually and then as a group. The activity sheet can be used for this.
- Each child should then write a sentence about the book which is intended to persuade someone who does not know the book to read it. Each group can then work on a presentation to the whole class in which each member of the group has to make a positive statement about the book. In the early stages this can just be to read out their sentence. Later, the children can develop the presentation to persuade others to read their book (such as producing posters to promote the book).
- After the presentation, the rest of the class could ask the group questions about the book.

# Opinions about a book

Name of book: ______________________________

Author: ______________________________

| Likes | Dislikes | Other comments |
|---|---|---|
| | | |

You should read this book because ______________________________

______________________________

______________________________

______________________________

______________________________

______________________________

NOW

- Find another book by the same author, or with a similar story-line.

# Traditional stories – Ideas page

## Aims

- To recognise particular structural and organisational features in traditional stories.

## Activities

- Ask the children to use the school or class library to collect folk-tales, such as *Beauty and the Beast* and *The Frog Prince*, which involve humans transforming into animals. Let them work in pairs or groups to take one of these tales and break it down into elements of the tale.
- They could record:
  - the setting, time and place
  - the characteristics of the main characters
  - the main problem to be overcome.

## Starting points

- Brainstorm and record the fairy stories and folk-tales that the children know.
- Record the characteristics of a prince, a princess and a dragon.
- Read a non-traditional fairy story such as *The Paper Bag Princess* by Robert Munsch or *The Practical Princess* by Jay Williams. Discuss the elements of the tale that do not conform to the traditional folk-tale. Discuss those that do.

| | Traditional Princess | Elizabeth |
|---|---|---|
| What happens | Captured by dragon.<br>Rescued by prince.<br>Marries prince. | Prince captured by dragon.<br>Outwits dragon and rescues prince.<br>Does not marry prince. |
| About the character | Beautiful, long, blonde hair. | Short hair. |

- Discuss other devices used in traditional stories, such as magic and trickery.

## Extension activities

- Find books that contain 'pourquoi' or 'why' stories such as Ted Hughes' *How the Whale Became* and Verna Aardema's *Why Mosquitoes Buzz in People's Ears*. Ask the children to discuss the elements of the tale with a partner or in a group.
- Let them produce their own 'how' or 'why' story.
- Read creation stories from one particular country or faith. Able readers could compare these with stories from another country and record the common elements in them. Children with access to folk-tales, myths and legends from other countries can be encouraged to share these with the class.
- Take a well-known fairy story and change the point of view of the storyteller by mixing up the characters, altering the theme or telling what happens next. Picture books, such as Jon Scieszka's *The Frog Prince Continued* and *The True Story of the Three Little Pigs* as well as Babette Cole's *Prince Cinders*, could be used as models for children's own writing. More able and confident readers could look at books such as Brian Keaney's *No Need for Heroes* which retells the story of *Theseus and the Minotaur* from Ariadne's point of view.

# Fabulous monsters

All these monsters can be found in Greek myths and legends.

- Find out:
  - who killed the Hydra
  - who killed the Gorgon
  - who killed the Minotaur
  - which gate Cerberus guarded.

The Hydra
nine-headed serpent

The Gorgon
woman's head with snakes for hair

The Minotaur
half man/half bull

Cerberus
three-headed dog, guarding the entrance to hell

- Think of some words that storytellers use to make these monsters horrible and frightening.

NOW

- Find monsters in other stories.

# What is fantasy? – Ideas page

## Aims

- To use modelling as a strategy for comprehension of a written passage.
- To identify different forms of modern fantasy stories.
- To raise awareness about particular children's authors who write modern fantasy fiction.

## Activities

- Read aloud the extract from *The Worst Witch*. The children should make a picture of the Witches' Academy in their minds.
- Explain that the children should use the author's description of the Academy as instruction for what to draw.

- In pairs, they could then compare the completed pictures. Examine the extent to which they used the words in the passage, which words were unfamiliar to them, if they used their imagination to add things to the written description and how much they have drawn from fantasy and how much from reality.
- The children should find other books by the same author and/or in the same series and see if they can find any patterns in the writing.

## Starting points

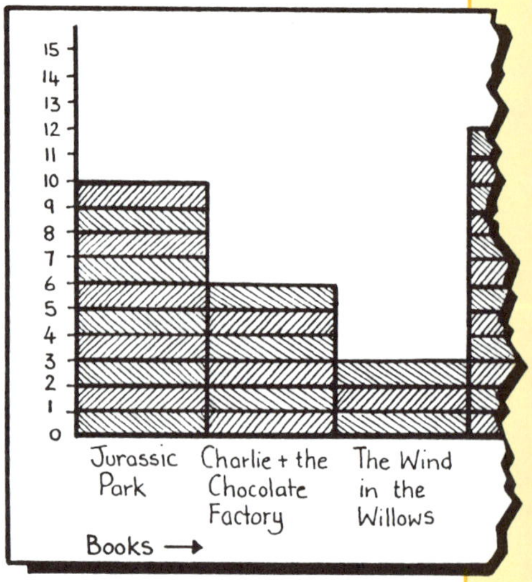


- Ask the children to write down their five favourite books. Make a graph of the top ten.
- Identify any that could be described as modern fantasy stories, for example *The Chronicles of Narnia*, *Charlotte's Web* and *Charlie and the Chocolate Factory*.
- Examine fantasy elements in the stories and compare these with ways in which the authors have made the story believable.
- Look at the variety of forms of modern fantasy. For example:

**Animal fantasy** – *Paddington* by Michael Bond
*Mrs Frisby and the Rats of NIMH* by Robert C O'Brien
*Wind in the Willows* by Kenneth Graham
**Toys** – *The Doll's House* by Rumer Godden
*The Indian in the Cupboard* by Lynne Reid Banks
**Amazing people** – *Pippi Lonstocking* by Astrid Lindgren
*Matilda* by Roald Dahl
**Amazing worlds** – *The Wizard of Oz* by L Frank Baum
*The Borrowers* by Mary Norton
**Supernatural** – *The Ghost of Thomas Kempe* by Penelope Lively
**Timeshifts** – *Tom's Midnight Garden* by Philippa Pearce
**Quests** – *The Hobbit* by JRR Tolkien

- Knowledge of different authors and their books is considered to be a reading skill. Ask the children to identify their favourite authors of fantasy books.

## Extension activities

- Working with the children, make a map to show an extraordinary world that appears in a book. If the children know the story well they could make a key which places events in the story.
- Make a collection of modern fantasy books that have illustrated covers. Put them into sets. Let the children discover that many books fit into more than one set – extraordinary worlds and imaginary kingdoms, fantastic animals, personified toys and dolls, eccentric and preposterous situations, magical powers, supernatural stories and science fiction books.
- Ask them to look at comics they enjoy and to identify fantasy story-lines in these.

 

# Miss Cackle's academy

- Finish the drawing of the outside of Miss Cackle's Academy for Witches.
- Make a note of all the things that you will need to include.

'Miss Cackle's Academy stood at the top of a high mountain surrounded by a pine forest. It looked more like a prison than a school, with its gloomy grey walls and turrets. Sometimes you could see the pupils on their broomsticks flitting like bats above the playground wall, but usually the place was half hidden in mist, so that if you glanced up at the mountain you would probably not notice the building was there at all.'

From: The Worst Witch by Jill Murphy

NOW

- Label the important parts of your picture.

# Faction – Ideas page

## Aims

- To discuss the differences between fact and fiction, using contemporary realistic fiction.
- To develop awareness of the use of narrative fiction to convey factual information.
- To develop an understanding of story structure and story language.

## Activities

- In groups or pairs, let the children discuss what is likely to happen next in the story. Younger children could look at the characters, setting and the atmosphere first before moving on to prediction. The children should be able to justify their predictions and provide evidence for them from the extract. More able children should be encouraged to keep the story as realistic as possible. Ask younger and less able children to draw what they think might happen next.
- Different predictions for the same story could be word processed and displayed with a short summary of the book.

## Starting points

- Make a collection of fiction books with which the children are familiar.
- Let them discuss in groups the books that they have enjoyed and would recommend to others.

- As a class, discuss differences in fiction books and let the children group the books according to whether they are:
  - picture books
  - traditional literature, such as fairy stories and folk-tales, myths and legends
  - historical fiction
  - modern fantasy stories
  - contemporary realistic fiction.
- Can the children identify whether the fiction books that they enjoy come into a particular category?
- Read aloud an extract from a contemporary realistic fiction book, such as *The Pinballs* by Betsy Byars, *The Stories Julian Tells* by Ann Cameron and *The Jaws of the Dragon* by Alan Gibbons. Let the children look at the difference between this sort of book (which reflects life today) and a fairy story or fantasy story. Highlight the close links between fact and fiction in these cases and how the plot remains within the realms of the possible.

## Extension activities

- The children could examine short opening extracts from several books and compare stories that start slowly with those where the action begins immediately.
- As a class, look at the ways in which the author has used language to create the mood of the story.
- In groups, examine fiction books that take up particular themes, for example school stories, family stories or survival stories.

- Read the children the picture book *Alexander and the Terrible, Horrible, No Good, Very Bad Day* by Judy Viorst. The children could list some of the terrible things that could be put into their own 'terrible day' book.

 

# What's next?

- Read the following extract which comes from the beginning of Journey to Jo'burg by Beverley Naidoo.

Naledi and Tiro were worried. Their baby sister Dineo was ill, very ill. For three days now, Nono their granny had been trying to cool her fever with damp cloths placed on her little head and body.

'We must get Mma (mother), or Dineo is going to die!' said Naledi.

'But how?' Tiro was bewildered. Their mother worked and lived in Johannesburg, more than 300 kilometres away.

'We can get to the big road and walk,' Naledi replied calmly.

It was clear that Naledi had made up her mind – and Tiro knew his sister.

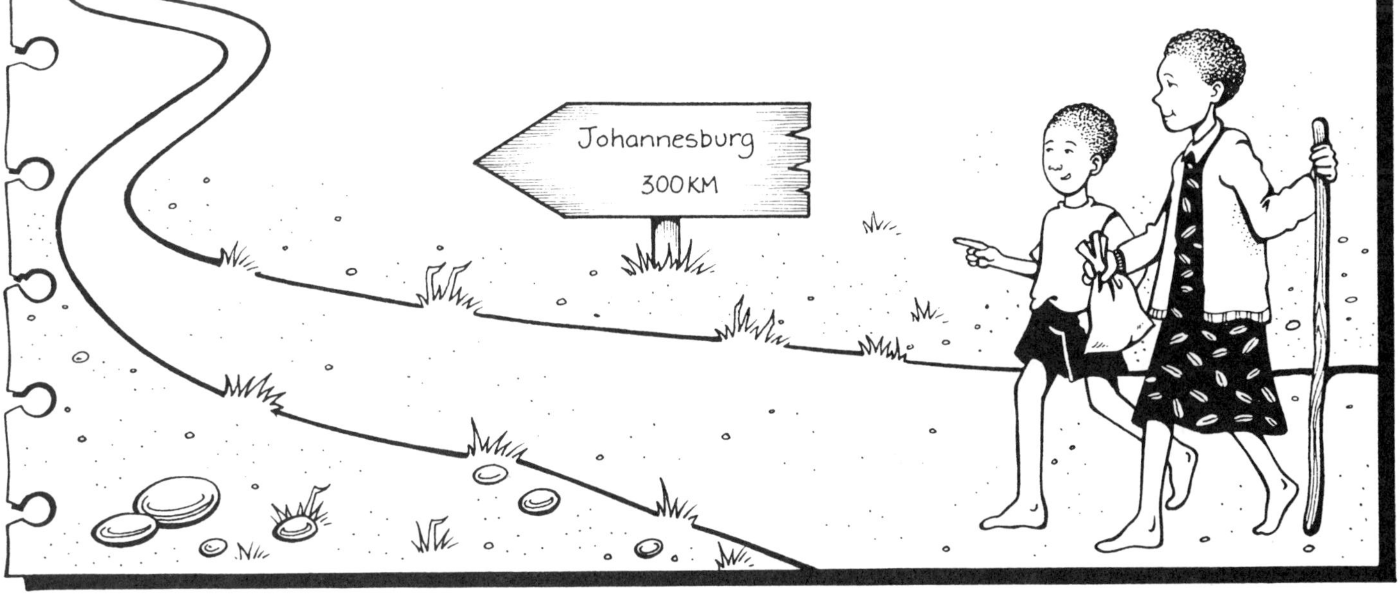


- Who are the main characters in the story?
- In what country is the story taking place?
- What do you think is going to happen next and why?
- Why do you think that?
- Could the story with your ending really happen?
- What type of story-book is this?

# Long ago – Ideas page

## Aims

- To read and sequence events into a meaningful format.
- To identify historical fiction as a form of literature.

## Activities

- Let the children work with a collection of picture books about a specific period in the past, such as Roy Gerard's books on the Victorians. Let them choose one book and record what clues the pictures provide about how people lived in the past.
- Make a simple time line recording the events that took place in the story.
- Introduce the activity sheet and explain to the children that they should sequence the events in this fictional story (the extract is taken from *In the lap of Athena* by Gill Goddard). They should record how they know that this story is written about the past.

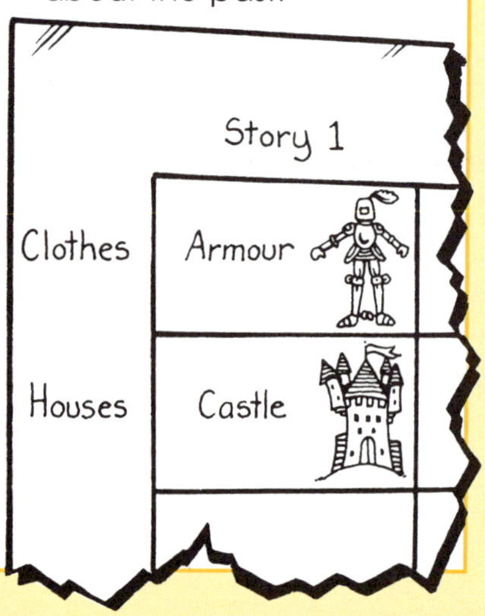


## Starting points

- Show the children a short video extract from a television historical drama or comedy.
- Explore how they know that the story is set in the past.

| Clues from the past | Examples from (title of book/video): |
|---|---|
| Clothes of characters | |
| Names of characters | |
| Setting in which the events take place | |
| Work the characters are doing | |
| Famous historical events taking place | |
| Language used – unfamiliar words, ways in which people greet each other and so on | |
| Other clues – music, transport used, games played, food and so on | |

- Discuss with the children how authors and producers of historical drama find out about the past through the use of non-fiction.

## Extension activities

- The children can use the class or school library to find non-fiction books about the same period in the past.
- They could find a picture or photograph in one of these books and write a story about something that might have happened.
- More able readers could find and read other historical fiction from the same period and record the references made to clothing, food, transportation, language and so on. This will help them to evaluate the most authentic story.
- Make a collection of resources which could be linked to the book, such as:
  - recipes from the book's time
  - a time line of the book's events
  - a map of the actual or imagined setting
  - a letter, diary or log that could have been written by one of the characters
  - a list of other fiction.
- Research and list authors who have written historical fiction.

# Long ago and far away

- Cut out the sections and put them in logical sequence.

One of the boys fell awkwardly and twisted his arm. I begged the Games Master to let me take his place. For a long moment I thought he wouldn't agree, but then Sicinnus nodded so he hoisted me up on the back of the black stallion.

I urged the horse on, harder and harder, driving my heels into his sides and desperately trying to stay on at the same time.

It took a while to bring the horse under my command but I was able to take my place at the starting line for the next race. It was a sprint, the length of the stadium, no turns, easy.

Today at last, Sicinnus, our slave tutor, let me try horse-racing. We were at the palaestra this afternoon when the horses were brought in to allow the riders a chance to practise their races for the Games.

We crossed the line first.

- Where do you think these events were taking place?
- When do you think they were taking place?
- What evidence do you have from the text?

# *Rap, rhyme and rhythm – Ideas page*

## Aims

- To raise awareness of sound effects used in poetry, such as rhyme, alliteration, onomatopoeia and repetition.
- To use listening and reading skills to develop phonic knowledge.
- To understand the use of metaphor in poetry.

## Activities

- In groups the children should make collections of poems to share with other groups. One group could look at poems with a strong sense of rhythm while another group could concentrate on poems that they enjoy, but that do not rhyme. More able children could look at ways in which other aspects of sound such as alliteration (repetition of initial consonant sounds) and assonance (repetition of particular vowel sounds) have been used.
- Ask them to read aloud and use one of the poetry extracts on the activity sheet to model their own poem on. Display poems about colour on appropriate coloured paper.
- Each child's favourite poem could be taped and/or a collection made in a class book.

## Starting points

- If the children have not heard much poetry or do not know many nursery rhymes, poetry can be introduced with street rhymes, raps and jump-rope rhymes. Ask them to make a collection of these using a Mother Goose Treasury and use this as a base for widening their experience of rhyme and sound.
- Choose a selection of short poems that have a strong rhythm, for example Eloise Greenfield's *Rope Rhyme* and Stevenson's *Windy Nights*, and read these aloud.
- Give the children an opportunity to read these poems to each other and then present them to a larger group. Some words may need to be explained but the emphasis of the activity should be on the sound and overall meaning of the poem. Provide time for the children to read and re-read the same poem, so that they begin to 'take possession' of it and can see how reading a poem is different from reading a story or information book.
- Let them take turns to choose a poem to read out or put on a display board as a special 'Poem a Day' feature.

## Extension activities

- In pairs, read and share poems such as Paul Fleishman's *Poems for Two Voices*, or work in small groups with poems such as Michael Rosen's *I'm the Youngest in our House*.
- The children could select a word picture from a poem and make a quick sketch of it.
- They could learn a favourite poem by heart.

- Collect poems that could be used in greetings cards for different occasions.

 

# Word magic

Below is part of a poem by Edwin Morgan.

- Can you finish it with some of your own nonsense rhyming words?

The Computer's first Christmas Card

jollymerry
hollyberry
jollyberry
merryholly
happyjolly
jellyberry

In the poem below, Mary O'Neill uses metaphors to say something is something else.

What is White?

White is a dove
And lily of the valley
And a puddle of milk
Spilled in an alley
A ship's sail
A kite's tail.

- Write a poem like this about another colour. What is ..?

# *Story poems –* **Ideas page**

## Aims

- To use inference and deduction through looking at narrative poems.
- To develop the skills of comprehension and research.

## Starting points

- Read Robert Browning's *The Pied Piper of Hamelin* to the class, or with younger children one of A A Milne's narrative poems, such as *Missing* or *The King's Breakfast*. Discuss and record initial responses to the story.
- Discuss the literary language used by the author, for example similes and metaphors.
- Display other narrative poems that have been made into picture books such as *The Highway Man* by Alfred Noyes, *The Owl and the Pussy-Cat* by Edward Lear, *Hiawatha* by Henry Wadsworth Longfellow and *The Legend of William Tell* by Terry Small.

## Activities

- Read and re-read the two poetry extracts on the activity sheet. Discuss what stories they are telling and the feelings that the language used creates.
- Ask the children to make a bookmark to record the title of a narrative poem that a particular classmate might enjoy. On one side they should write the title and illustrate it, on the other a review of the poem.

## Extension activities

- Choose another narrative poem and ask the children, in pairs, to focus on one character at a specific point in the poem, such as Aunt Jobiska in Edward Lear's *The Pobble who has no Toes*. They could write what they think she is thinking about at that moment in time.
- Let members of a group illustrate different episodes from one of the poems and display them during a rehearsed reading of the poem.
- Challenge them to change the form of the poem, so that the story is retold as an item on the news, a newspaper report or a record in a diary.
- Make a frieze of one narrative poem. Each child or pair of children can be given a section of the poem to copy out and illustrate.

# Story poems

This is the first part of a poem that tells the story of a battle in the Crimean War.

The Charge of the Light Brigade

Half a league, half a league
Half a league onward,
All in the valley of Death
Rode the six hundred
'Forward the Light Brigade!
Charge for the gun!' he said:
Into the valley of Death
Rode the six hundred.

- Why do you think the poet calls it 'the valley of Death'?
- What is a league?

Here are two verses from a poem by Shel Silverstein.

I'll tell you the story of Jimmy Jet
And you know what I tell you is true.
He loved to watch his TV set
Almost as much as you.

He watched all day, he watched all night
Till he grew pale and lean,
From 'The Early Show' to 'The Late Late Show'
And all the shows between.

- What title would you give the poem?
- What do you think happens to Jimmy Jet?
- Write another verse for the poem.

# Library power – Ideas page

## Aims

- To raise awareness of the variety of information texts available in libraries.
- To develop skills in locating different sources of information.

## Starting points

- Find a library that will allow a visit from you and the class. Identify the resources and services available for children's use. See what is available in addition to books (for example videos, tapes, CD-ROM, magazines, children's story projects).
- Let the children find out about joining a library and what activities the library organises for children, for example:
  - what they need to have before borrowing books
  - the amount of books that they can borrow
  - what other items can be borrowed
  - the length of time for which books can be borrowed
  - the opening and closing times of the library
  - if there is a fee to join the library
  - what holiday activities (if any) are organised.
- Compare the school and class libraries with the local library. Let the children draw a plan of the school/class library, indicating where information materials may be found. Look at the ways in which books are sorted into reference, fiction and non-fiction books.

## Activities

- Ask the children to complete the activity sheet. Discuss with them any titles that they are unsure of. Have they understood the differences between the categories?
- In pairs, let them choose a subject that they are both interested in and use the subject index in the library catalogue to locate books on the topic. Let them write down the titles of the books that they think look most interesting to read.
- Ask the children to use an encyclopaedia to find out what Melville Dewey was famous for.
- List a book for each of the following categories.

| Categories | Numbers | List one book for each |
|---|---|---|
| Generalities | 000-099 | |
| Philosophy | 100-199 | |
| Religion | 200-299 | |
| Social Sciences | 300-399 | |
| Language | 400-499 | |
| Sciences | 500-599 | |
| Technology | 600-699 | |
| Arts | 700-799 | |
| Literature | 800-899 | |
| Geography and History | 900-999 | |

## Extension activities

- In small groups, the children should return books that have been taken out from the library to the right shelves.
- The children could design a poster to show very young children how to care for books.

# Library power!

**Reference**
These are books that are used in the library and not taken out. Reference books have facts and subject areas.

**Fiction**
These are books written in a make-believe way. The writer uses imagination to write. These books are placed in alphabetical order by the last name of the writer.

**Non-fiction**
These books have true stories and facts. Non-fiction books are placed on the shelves using a special numbering system called the Dewey Decimal System.

- Write on the spine of each book whether it is a fiction book (F), reference book (R) or non-fiction book (N).

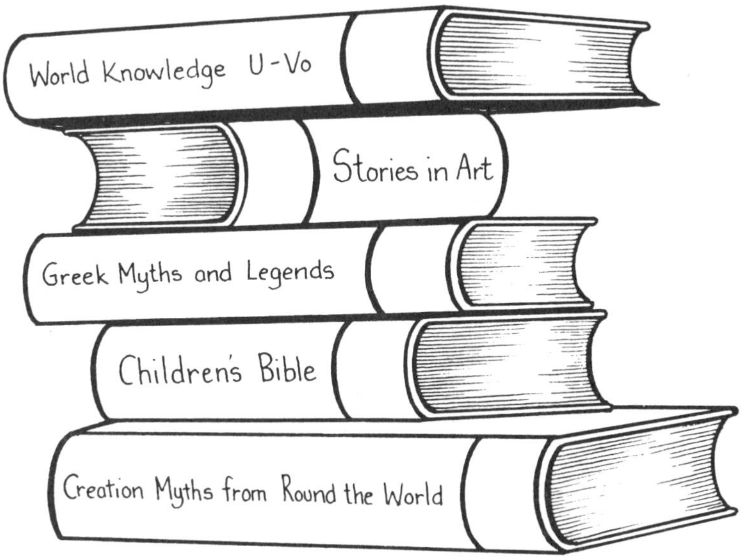


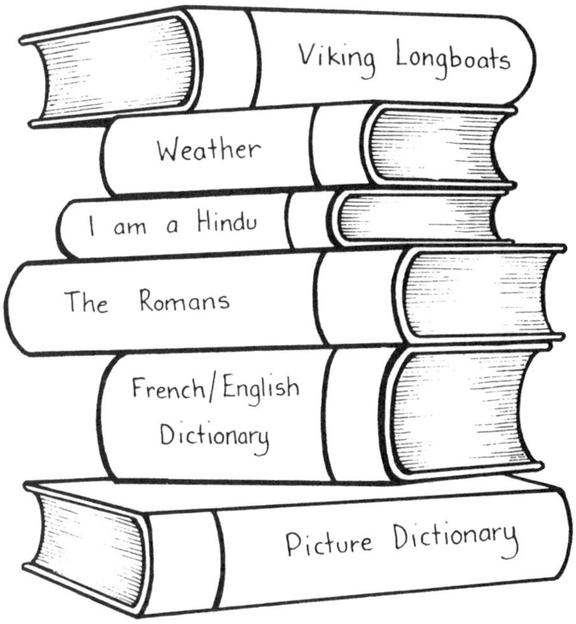


NOW

- Which books might fit into more than one category?

# Alphabetical order – Ideas page

## Aims

- To use knowledge of the alphabet to help find facts quickly in reference materials such as dictionaries, encyclopaedias and telephone directories.
- To identify that some non-fiction books are organised in alphabetical order.

## Starting points

- Play some alphabet games to reinforce understanding of the alphabet – oral games such as 'My mother went to market' and board games such as 'Scrabble'.

- Ask the children to line up in alphabetical order, either using forenames or surnames.
- Collect street names from the surrounding area and collate them into alphabetical order.
- Try to get the whole class involved in creating alphabet poetry, for example:
  **A** was an apple pie,
  **B** bit it,
  **C** cut it,
  **D** dealt it and so on.
- Put fiction books into alphabetical order according to the surname of the author.
- Identify other areas of the library where alphabetical order is used as a means of storing resources so that they can be found easily.

## Activities

- Explain that the first activity on the sheet is valid, since this might be done for an index or glossary of a book on tennis.
- Look at reference guide words used at the top of pages in dictionaries. Ask the children how such guide words work and if they can think of any other reference books that have guide words.
- Let them choose a double-page spread in a dictionary, write the guide words down and then list six words that can be found on the page.

## Extension activities

- Ask the children to write the letters **a** to **z** in a column. After each letter, they should write a word beginning with that letter. Dictionaries should be used to help. These words could be linked to a theme being studied in history or geography or an issue about which the children are concerned, such as pollution.
- Graeme Base's picture alphabet book *Animalia* could be used as a model for an alliterative alphabet book. He depicts fantastic creatures and objects whose names commence with the given letter and are captioned by alliterative phrases such as 'diabolical dragons daintily devouring delicious delicacies'.
- Lists of words could be related to current themes being studied, for example Space:
  'sun', 'satellite', 'Saturn', 'solar', 'stars', 'Sputnik'.
- Children could create letter-string lists, such as ten words that start with **tri**.

 

# Alphabetical order

Television commentators often use specialist words in their reports. These words are often used in a tennis commentary.

- Put them into alphabetical order.

volley
smash
baseline
lob
drop
service
grip
rankings
backhand
doubles

- Where might you find them printed in alphabetical order?

Reference books like dictionaries have Alphabetical Guide Words at the top of each page. They give clues about what other words will be found on the page.

- Circle the correct answers. The first one is done for you

| Guide words | Entry word | Choices |
|---|---|---|
| cardinal–cast | car | On Page - Turn Back - Turn Forward |
| platform–plumber | pill | On Page - Turn Back - Turn Forward |
| glacial–gnaw | gloss | On Page - Turn Back - Turn Forward |
| might–mine | mistletoe | On Page - Turn Back - Turn Forward |
| employ–endure | enemy | On Page - Turn Back - Turn Forward |
| sofa–sound | snore | On Page - Turn Back - Turn Forward |

# *Look it up* – *Ideas page*

## Aims

- To become familiar with the information that dictionaries provide.
- To consolidate knowledge of alphabetical order and to extend vocabulary.

## Starting points

- Ask the children to provide reasons for using a dictionary

**Why use a dictionary?**
- for spelling words
- pronouncing words
- discover what part of speech a word is
- find out meanings
- find origin of a word

- Look at the different types of dictionaries kept in the classroom, including picture dictionaries and adult dictionaries.
- Demonstrate how to 'read' the dictionary, explaining guidewords, punctuation, different fonts and word variations. More able children could look at dictionaries that show the origins of words, parts of speech and pronunciation.
- Explore the different elements of dictionaries, such as the introduction, abbreviations and the explanation of phonetic pronunciation used.

## Activities

- In groups, let the children make a collage of homophones, using a dictionary to check definitions for words that sound the same but are spelled differently, for example bear and bare, ball and bawl, cheap and cheep, dessert and desert.

- Ask them to use a dictionary to find words that have more than one meaning such as: 'wooden club used in cricket'/ 'winged mouse-like animal that flies at night'.
Answer: bat.

## Extension activities

- Explore different types of dictionaries. This can be one way of introducing children to another script.
- Use a foreign language dictionary to find the word for 'hello'.
- Let the children catalogue the dictionaries in the library by title and publisher.
- The children could use a dictionary to find the origin of words such as 'crêpe', 'soprano', 'judo' and 'politics'.

- Make a 'word-of-the-day' Calendar; for example

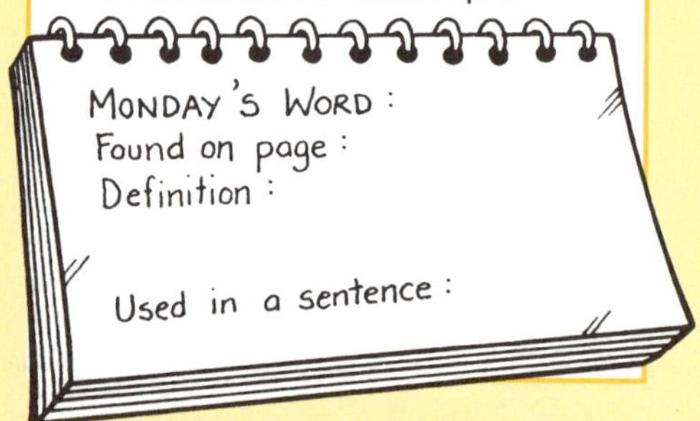

# Dictionary skills

The Water Cycle

Water is the only substance that is found in the form of a liquid, a solid and a gas. When water evaporates it changes from a liquid to a gas and rises into the air. Clouds are water. The higher you go, the colder the air is. When water vapour rises the cold air makes the vapour form droplets which hang in the air as mist. This is a cloud. This water returns to earth again as rain or snow. This is called the water cycle. Ice is frozen water.

- Find the words below in the text and underline them. Guess the meaning of the word and then use a dictionary to check the meaning.

| | Guess | Meaning |
|---|---|---|
| liquid | | |
| solid | | |
| gas | | |
| evaporate | | |
| vapour | | |
| droplets | | |
| mist | | |

# Expanding the vocabulary – Ideas page

## Aims

- To use a thesaurus to extend vocabulary.
- To note the meanings of any newly-encountered words.

## Starting points

- Read Jill Murphy's *On the Way Home* to the children and get them to write down the different words that she has used to introduce dialogue such as 'said', 'asked', 'exclaimed', 'gasped' and 'cried'.
- Role-play sentences using each of these and discuss the differences between the words. Which words are most like 'said'?
- Introduce the word 'synonym' and the idea that a thesaurus contains words that are similar in meaning to a headword, for example, fight: 'action', 'attack', 'battle', 'bout', 'boxing match', 'brawl', 'clash', 'combat', 'competition', 'contest', 'counter-attack', 'duel', 'encounter', 'engagement', 'feud', 'hostilities', 'joust', 'quarrel', 'raid', 'rivalry', 'row', 'scramble', 'scrap', 'scuffle', 'squabble', 'strife', 'struggle', 'tussle', 'vendetta', 'war'.
- Look at the differences between some of these words, such as 'fight' and 'scrap', 'fight' and 'battle' and so on.
- With the children, examine the structure of a thesaurus, identifying headwords, reasons for numbering and different fonts.

## Activities

- Ask the children to use the thesaurus to create an alphabetical list of synonyms, identifying one for each letter of the alphabet.
- Let them select a page from their reading book and write down any adjectives that they can find. They can then use the thesaurus to find an alternative that still keeps the sense of the text.

## Extension activities

- Ask the children to make a collection of advertisements and use the thesaurus to find different adjectives to describe the products.
- The children could design an advertisement to sell an unwanted Christmas present. The thesaurus can be used to find as many positive adjectives as they can. They could start by looking up the word 'beautiful'.

- Get them to type a poem on to the computer and use the computer thesaurus to change some of the words. The children could read it aloud and explore what difference the word changes have made to the sound and rhythm of the poem as well as its meaning.

 

# Something different

- Use the thesaurus to find words to replace the following: 'fabulous', 'marvellous', 'amazing', 'delicious', 'delightful', 'smooth'.

- Use the thesaurus to find another word to use instead of 'nice'.

It's a nice day. ______________________

This is a nice jacket. ______________________

The food tastes nice. ______________________

We had a nice time. ______________________

The holiday was nice. ______________________

He's a nice swimmer. ______________________

## Using encyclopaedias – Ideas page

### Aims

- To appreciate that an encyclopaedia is one of the first places to look for information.
- To identify which volume of an encyclopaedia should be used to obtain information on a specific topic.

### Starting points

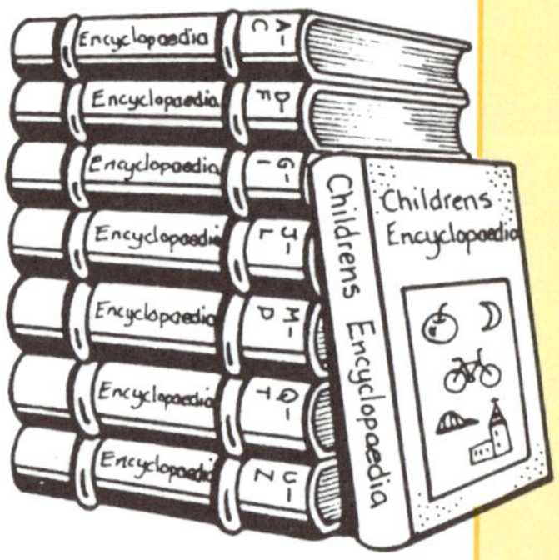


- Review the encyclopaedias in school with the children. Identify the differences between one-volume encyclopaedias and multi-volume encyclopaedias. Let the children explore the contents of encyclopaedias by looking up topics that they are particularly interested in.
- If possible use more than one encyclopaedia so that different texts on the same subject can be compared. Younger children could use a single volume such as the Dorling Kindersley *Children's Illustrated Encyclopaedia* or the Kingfisher *Children's Encyclopaedia.*
- More able readers can be introduced to the use of an index volume to help retrieval of information when the encyclopaedia contains several volumes such as the *Oxford Children's Encyclopaedia* and *Children's Britannica.* Information could be linked with history, geography or scientific themes being studied.

### Activities

- The children should complete the activity sheet and (in pairs) check each other's activity sheet to see whether they were in agreement about where the topics might be found. They should say which heading they chose as there is usually more than one option. For example, 'football' might be found under its own name or under the general heading 'sport'.
- Ask them to decide on a personal project or theme that they would like to investigate. They should write down what they already know about the topic and then list some questions that they would like to have answers for. Some children might find it useful to use the 'five w's' strategy as a starting point, for example:

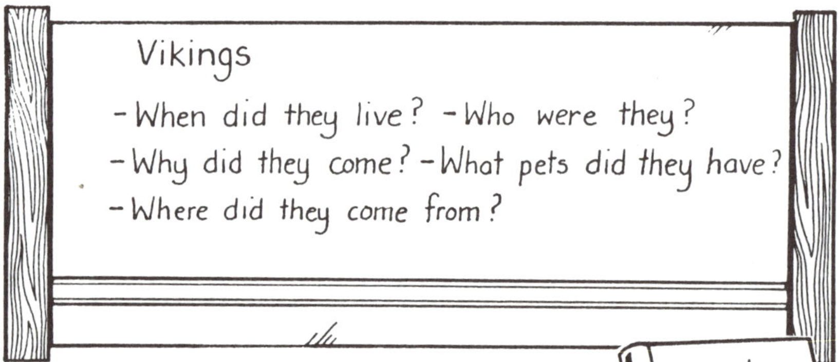


- Where the information is not available, the children should record the questions and identify other resources that might help, such as another encyclopaedia, non-fiction texts, atlases, wall-charts, posters, teletext, filmstrips or videos.

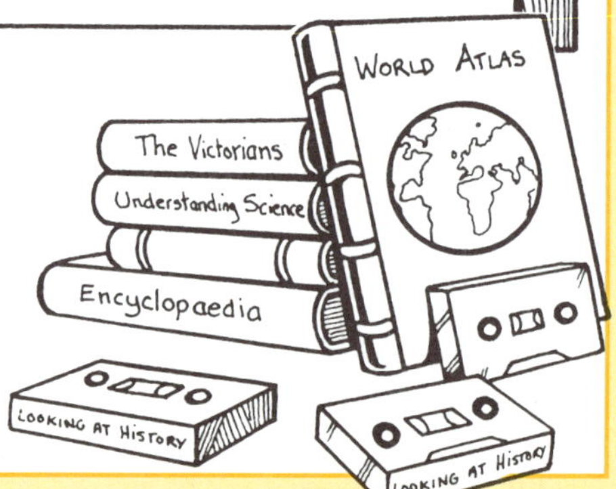


### Extension activities

- Ask the children to choose two countries that they would like to visit and to use the encyclopaedia to find out the capital city and interesting sights to see.

- They should use the encyclopaedia to make up general knowledge questions for a class quiz.
- Ask the children to create wordsearches on specialist subjects.

 

# Problem prowling

- In which volumes of the encyclopaedia would you find the main articles on these topics and under which heading?

| Topic | Volume | Heading |
|---|---|---|
| Football | 5 | Sport |
| Olympics | | |
| Space | | |
| Cats | | |
| America | | |
| Frankenstein | | |
| Rockets | | |
| Harriet Tubman | | |
| The Romans | | |
| Tutankhamun | | |

Some encyclopaedias are arranged in subject area:

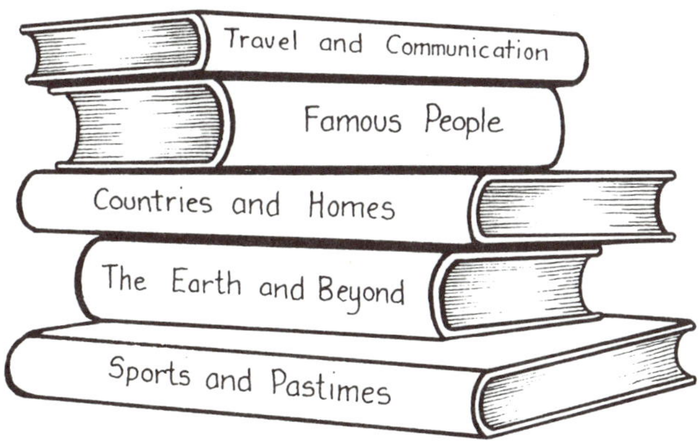


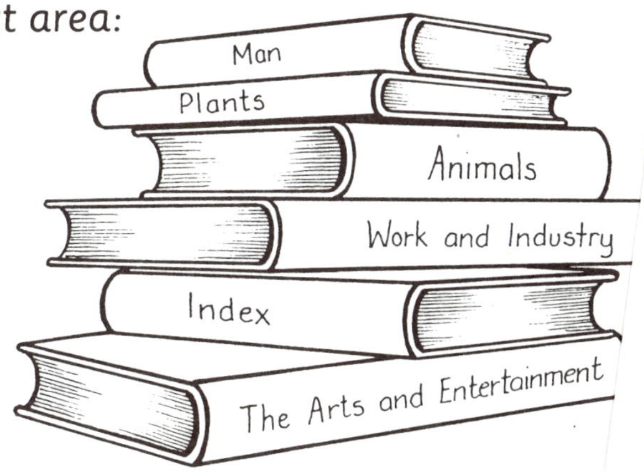


- In which volumes would you find main articles about these topics: 'Ships'; 'Inventors'; 'Rainforests'; 'Tigers'.

# *Narrative non-fiction –* ***Ideas page***

## Aims

- To recognise that some non-fiction books combine both narrative and information.

## Activities

- The activity sheet provides an extract from a narrative non-fiction text that incorporates a recipe for pineapple sherbet. Explain that they will often find factual information such as this in a story-book. They should develop the skill of extracting the cooking information from the story and rewriting it in recipe form.

- Use narrative non-fiction such as Lois Ehlert's *Growing Vegetable Soup* to show the children how a recipe can be made into a story. Do the same with a cake recipe for a special celebration.

## Starting points

- Make a collection of narrative non-fiction texts that use a story format to provide factual information about a particular topic. Some of these should be more challenging. Share one of these books with the class and compare it with an information text on the same subject. Titles could include: photographic essay books (such as *Ann in Bangladesh* by Nadia Kabeerand, *Doctor* by Tim Wood) and picture books (*The Shepherd Boy* by Kim Lewis, *The Day of Ahmed's Secret* by Florence Parry Heide & Judith Heide Gilliland).
- Work with the whole class using a Big Book such as *A House is a House for Me* by Mary Ann Hoberman and compare this with an information text on homes.
- Read with the children Janet and Allan Ahlberg's *Starting School* and use it as a model for writing an introduction for someone new starting in their class.
- Let the children bring in from home any books that they think come into this category of narrative non-fiction and explore the difference between known fact and fiction.

| Title of book: *The Day of Ahmed's Secret* | | |
|---|---|---|
| Fact | Fiction | We do not know |
| Child labour exists in Egypt | Ahmed's secret was the loudest sound in the world | Does Ahmed exist? |
| Some children cannot read or write | | Ahmed learned to write. |

## Extension activities

- Show the children a video that looks at how a particular children's author writes a book (such as the *Author Video Bank* from the Children's Book Foundation). They should write this up into a story and compare it with biographies and autobiographies written about children's authors. Ruth Thompson's *How a Book is Made* could be used to follow this up as it tells the story of book production from the initial idea through to the final product.
- Provide either biographies or extracts from biographies of people the children are studying in history. They could record important events of that person's life on a time line.

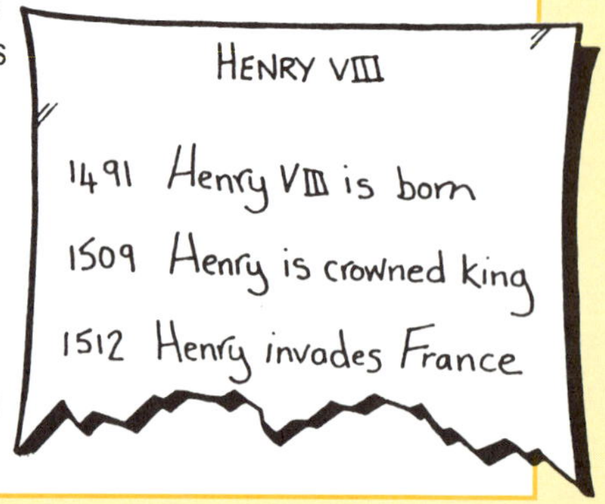

# Fiction to fact

- *Read the text below and then present the information again giving clear instructions on how to make Caribbean pineapple sherbet.*

Marios loved it when he went to stay with his grandmother. She always spoilt him and he would help her to make the tea. His favourite was Caribbean pineapple sherbet and his gran used pineapple, orange juice, milk and sugar to make it. Sometimes Marios helped her. They would heat up a pint of milk and then stir in 250g of sugar. When the sugar had dissolved they would put the mixture into the refrigerator to cool down. While they were waiting for it to go cold they would chop up the pineapple and squeeze all the juice out of one orange. Marios liked doing this because he enjoyed eating the inside of the orange, when all the juice had gone. The pineapple and milk would be mixed together and put into the fridge to freeze. Once the mixture had set his gran would get it out of the fridge and put it into her blender to mix again. It would have to go back into the fridge to re-freeze before they could eat it.

Ingredients:-

Method:-

# Surveying information books – Ideas page

## Aims

- To develop strategies to use in accessing information.
- To develop the ability to assess whether an information book will be useful for a specific project or theme.
- To raise awareness of structural guiders in information books and to develop the ability to use them.

## Starting points

- Make a collection of books on different topics, either related to class topics already being studied or topics of particular interest to the children. Working with small groups, give each child one of these information books and ask them to find out what it is about.
- Ask the children what their book is about. Note those who have used structural guiders, such as details on the back of the book, the contents page and so on, as a clue to context and those who just started to read the book from start to finish.
- List those structural guiders that the children can identify as being useful in finding out what is in the book. Point out any that appear in the books, but have not been noted by the children.

## Activities

- Let the children collect some information books about any special interests or hobbies that they have. This can include books from home or the local library.

- Working in groups, according to interest, they should complete the matrix on the activity sheet for information books on a specific topic.
- When this has been done the children should review all the books and decide which one had the most useful structural guiders.

## Extension activities

- Discuss other criteria for choosing a good information book, such as an attractive layout, useful information and good illustrations.
- Let the children choose a topic and write down what they already know about it. They should then list questions about it and find the best books in the class/school/local library to answer them.

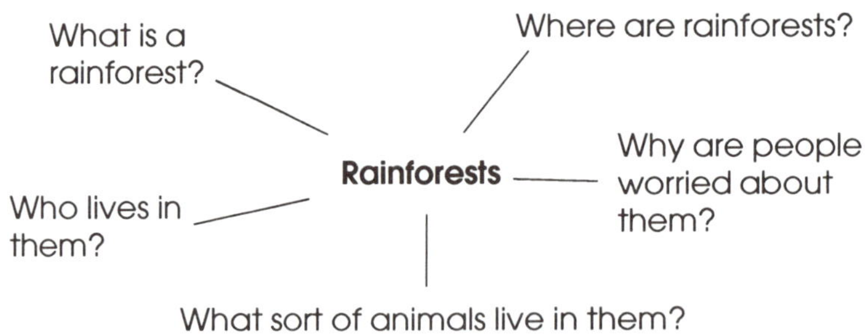


- The children could devise a poster that gives one or more answers to the questions and make a presentation on the topic using the poster.

# Surveying books

Title of Topic: ____________________

| Structural guider | Title of book | | | | | |
|---|---|---|---|---|---|---|
| Captions to photographs and illustrations | | | | | | |
| Chapters | | | | | | |
| Colour | | | | | | |
| Contents page | | | | | | |
| Diagrams or graphs | | | | | | |
| Glossary | | | | | | |
| Illustrations | | | | | | |
| Index | | | | | | |
| Page numbers on all pages | | | | | | |
| Photographs | | | | | | |
| Picture on front cover | | | | | | |
| Sub-headings | | | | | | |
| Useful information on book cover | | | | | | |

# *How to find answers to questions –* ***Ideas page***

## Aims

- To develop the ability to evaluate texts for information retrieval.
- To raise questions that require the use of informational texts.

## Starting points

- Let the children identify different ways in which questions can be asked. The 'five w's' strategy can be used as a starting point – 'who', 'what', 'where', 'when', 'why'. The children should ask a question starting with each of these words. Initially they could start by asking a question to which they know the answer, then go on to ask a question to which they do not know the answer.
- Identify the type of questions that can be answered through the use of referenced texts, using an encyclopaedia as an initial starting point.

## Activities

- Do an author study – organise a class, group or individual study of a particular author of non-fiction books that are enjoyed by children, for example Terry Jennings and Ruth Thompson.
- Make a collection of books by the same author. Record any personal information about them that can be found inside the book or on the cover.
- Develop some questions to use to decide whether a book is a good one. For example:
  - Does the book cover the subject?
  - How good are the pictures?
  - Is the book easy to read?
  - How much actual information is included?
- Choose a book on one topic written by the chosen author and compare this with another book on the same topic by another author. For example *Senses* by Hazel Songhurst and *The Five Senses* by Dorine Barbey.

## Extension activities

- Invent a board game for either a chosen author or a particular topic. Question cards about the author and/or topic could be used to mark progress.

- The children could design a new book jacket for one of the books in the author collection, having considered what the contents of the book are and how this can be shown on the cover.
- They could also write to the author, care of the publisher's address, recording their enjoyment of his/her books.

# Question and answer sheet

My topic: ______________________________

Questions I need to find answers to:

1. Question: ______________________________

   Answer: ______________________________

2. Question: ______________________________

   Answer: ______________________________

3. Question: ______________________________

   Answer: ______________________________

I used ____________________ to help me find the answers.

# *Learning to scan –* *Ideas page*

## *Aims*

- To develop the ability to read information texts at speed.
- To identify and develop different reading strategies concentrating on scanning.

## *Activities*

- The two activities on the sheet are ideal for introducing both how we scan and why. Similar extracts can be culled from a variety of books for further practice.
- Let the children play with visual puzzle books, such as Martin Handford's *Where's Wally?* Ask them what skills they are using to find Wally. Lucy Micklethwait's *Numbers in Art* and *ABC in Art* are ideal for developing familiarity with famous works of art as well as for scanning them for specific objects.

## *Starting points*

- Make a collection of different sorts of texts including a newspaper, telephone directory, story-book and information text. Use these to discuss different types of reading strategy.

| Type of reading | Description | Purpose |
|---|---|---|
| 1. Detailed reading | reading the whole passage carefully | complete understanding |
| 2. Skimming | finding out what the passage is about | general impression |
| 3. Critical reading | separating fact and fiction | making up your mind |
| 4. Analytical reading | study the writer's technique and skills | appreciating style and structure |
| 5. Reading for enjoyment | reading at your own pace | pleasure |
| 6. Scanning | running your eye down the page looking for specific details | fact finding |

(From: *Power Pack* produced by the Library Association)

- Photocopy an extract from a telephone book and invite the children to find specific names and numbers. Explain that this is scanning and ask those who do it fastest to explain how they are doing it. Discuss why it is necessary to scan.
- Choose an information book linked to a theme being studied and select a double-page spread that covers a number of different ideas. Show children how to survey the text and raise questions about what the text may answer. Decide together what information the text provides and which are key sentences. If applicable look at different types of fonts used and the positioning of captions for pictures.

## *Extension activities*

- Working in pairs, let the children compile five 'can you find?' questions, based on a poster or photograph linked to a topic or theme in science, maths or geography. When they have finished they can swap questions and visual aids with another pair and use scanning skills to find objects.
- Ask them to find the phone number of the school, their own phone number or a friend's number in a telephone directory within a given time.
- Play games which help to improve scanning skills, for example 'Kim's game', which involves looking at a number of different artefacts on a tray for five minutes, covering them and then asking children to say or write what was on the tray.

# Scan it!

- Underline the dates and names of bicycles mentioned in the passage as quickly as you can.

The first pedal cycle was the so-called 'boneshaker' which first appeared in 1869. It was found that greater speeds could be achieved with a larger front wheel, so the 'penny-farthing' was introduced in 1879. The real popularity of cycling came with the invention of the 'safety bicycle' in the 1880s. The frame is like a modern bicycle and the pedals drive the back wheel via a chain and 'freewheeling' was now possible. At first the tyres were solid rubber, until in 1888 JB Dunlop invented the tyre with a blow-up inner tube.

- Underline, circle or highlight the following:
  - the number of moons for Saturn
  - the planet which is 5000km in diameter
  - the planet on which we live
  - the length of the year on Venus.

| Planet | Distance from the sun in millions of km | Length of year in Earth days | Diameter in km | Number of moons |
|---|---|---|---|---|
| Earth | 150 | 365 | 12756 | 1 |
| Jupiter | 778 | 4333 | 142700 | 16 |
| Mars | 228 | 687 | 6760 | 2 |
| Mercury | 58 | 88 | 5000 | 0 |
| Neptune | 4498 | 60188 | 49500 | 2 |
| Pluto | 5914 | 90700 | 3050 | 1 |
| Saturn | 1428 | 10759 | 120900 | 17 |
| Uranus | 2873 | 30685 | 46700 | 5 |
| Venus | 108 | 225 | 12180 | 0 |

- Why might some of the information in this table be wrong?

# Reading screens – Ideas page

## Aims

- To identify sources of written information on screens in school and at home.
- To develop skills in screen-reading for information.

## Activities

- The activity sheet introduces the type of screen layout, menus and information that the children might encounter. The questions aim to establish that they are confident in finding their way around the screen.
- Load a children's encyclopaedia or a CD-ROM related to a topic being carried out by the class. Show a pair of children how to work with it and then let them show another pair. Let each pair draw the computer screen at one particular point and label the different parts of the screen along the lines of the activity sheet.

- Working in pairs, give the children a couple of topic headings to find on screen and ask them to print off their findings from the computer or write them down in note form.

## Starting points

- Brainstorm the different monitors that the children already use inside and outside school, such as television, video, computers and video and computer games.
- Identify some of the different forms of written information that appear on a television screen (this could be carried out as a home-based activity and include Teletext and Cee-fax):

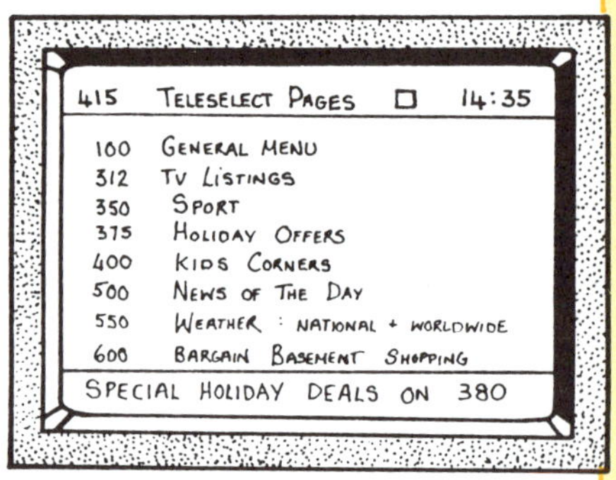


- Watch a video of a set of advertisements recorded at children's prime viewing time. Let the children list the advertisements and what written information is provided about the different products and services. Ask them how the writers of advertisements persuade people to buy.

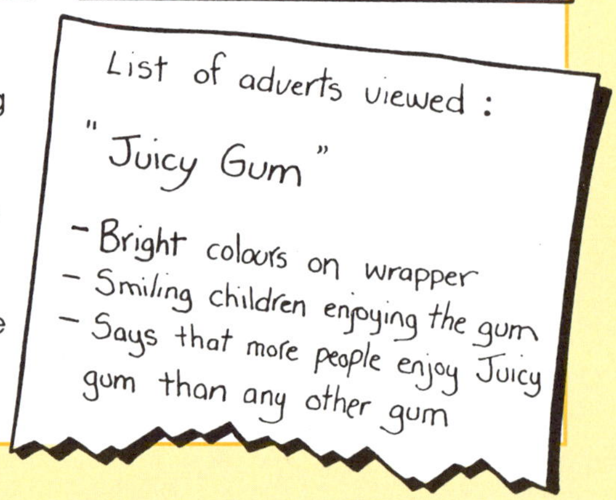


## Extension activities

- The program *Developing Tray* (LETTS, John Ruskin Street, London SE5 0PQ) can be used with small groups to enhance the reading of texts on screen. Poems are particularly successful.
- Look at the ways in which libraries put their books on to catalogue. OPAC (Online Public Access Catalogue) provides instructions on the screen to tell the user what to do.

# Reading the screen

Below is the first screen page of a CD-ROM about musical instruments.

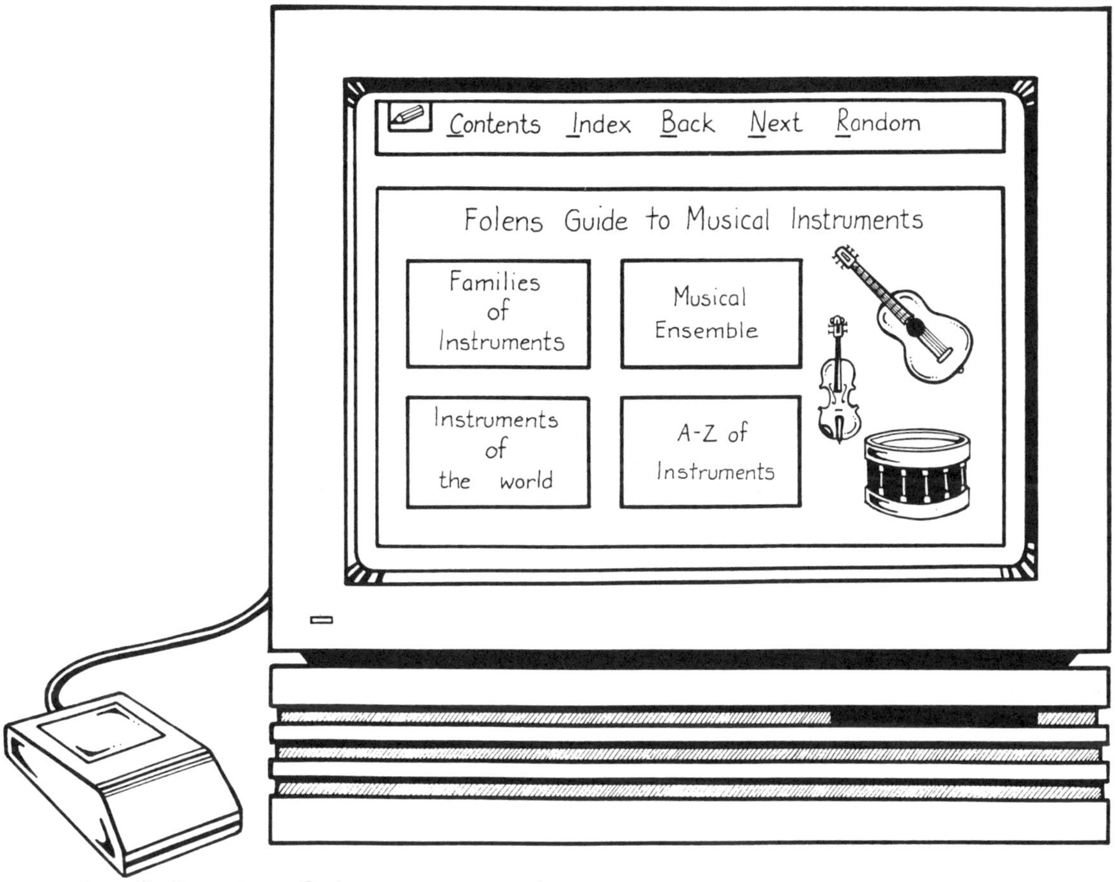


- What is the full title of the program? ______________________
- Why are some of the letters underlined? ______________________
- What would happen if you clicked on to Contents? ______________________
- If you wanted to find out more about the violin family which box would you click in to? ______________________
- If you wanted to find out about instruments that might be found in Africa which box would you use? ______________________

______________________________________________

NOW

- Draw a screen from a CD-ROM you enjoy using. Write down some instructions to help others to use the program.

# Community texts: Newspapers – Ideas page

## Aims

- To appreciate the different styles of language used for different purposes.
- To interpret content from a newspaper headline or subheading.

## Activities

- The activity sheet encourages the children to demonstrate their understanding of the brief and succinct nature of newspaper headlines.
- Follow this up by giving them a number of different headlines and asking them to decide what the story is. More able children could be given other more difficult newspaper articles with the headlines missing and could then make up their own headlines to fit the text.
- Ask the children to compare a tabloid newspaper with a broadsheet. Is one easier to read than the other?
- The children could compare the front page of one newspaper with the front page of another on the same day. Ask them if the pages look the same and whether the main story is the same. The children could examine whether the opinions are expressed in the same way and in what way the same story is treated differently.

## Starting points

- Let the children have copies of the same issue of a popular Sunday, daily or local newspaper and make a survey of it. For example:

| Page | Features |
|---|---|
| Page 1 | Main news story, information about scratch cards, second story. |
| Page 2 | Continue main story, contents, weather, three short stories, advert. |
| Page 3 | Three news stories. |

- Share the lead story to explore how the news is presented. Examine any subheadings and photographs that go with the text.
- After reading the first paragraph, the children could predict the rest of the story from the subheadings, before reading the article. They can then compare their predictions with the actual content and comment on how useful the subheadings and pictures are.
- Make a graph showing which newspapers the children have heard of.

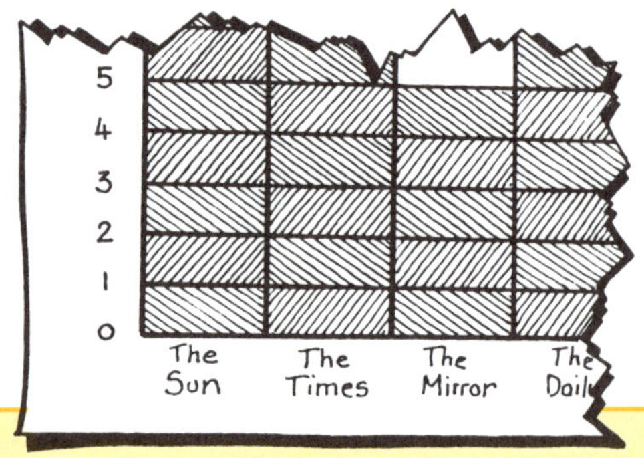


## Extension activities

- A newspaper brought into class could be used as a model for creating a class or school newspaper, with different children given responsibility for different stories.
- The children could make a collage of favourite cartoon characters such as 'Garfield' and could then compare different cartoon story-lines. This involves scanning different newspapers and will allow the children to become more familiar with them.
- Arrange for a small group to visit the local newspaper and report their visit back to the class.
- The children could look at the layout of the small fashion catalogues which often come as inserts in newspapers. What sort of adjectives and descriptive phrases are used to describe the clothes? If the children are studying a particular period in history, such as the Victorians, they could make a fashion catalogue of this era.

# Newspaper headlines

- *Write a short article for a newspaper under each headline.*

## WARD ST PUPILS QUALIFY

## Diamond hoard in playground

- *Write a headline for each of these articles.*

A tamper-proof car alarm drove people crazy when it resisted all their efforts to stop it blaring.
But police finally silenced it... by burying it in a flowerbed.

ROLL UP! Coarse fishing is open this weekend with seats in all parts after a three month break that barred sport in rivers and streams while some stillwaters and canals stayed open and others closed.

## Aims

- To develop skills in reading timetables and price charts, catalogues and brochures, junk mail and other written sources of information.
- To extend children's knowledge of local sources of information.

## Activities

- The activity sheet contains two different charts relating to travel and tourism. They are a good introduction to the way in which such information is presented to the public. If the children find these easy they could go on to use more detailed ones from travel agents.
- Let the children decide which part of the world they would like to visit and give them a specific sum of money that can be spent on the holiday itself.
- More able children could be encouraged to find additional information that would be needed to book the holiday, such as availability of flights and types of facilities available at their chosen destination. They could read and fill in the form found at the end of most travel brochures.

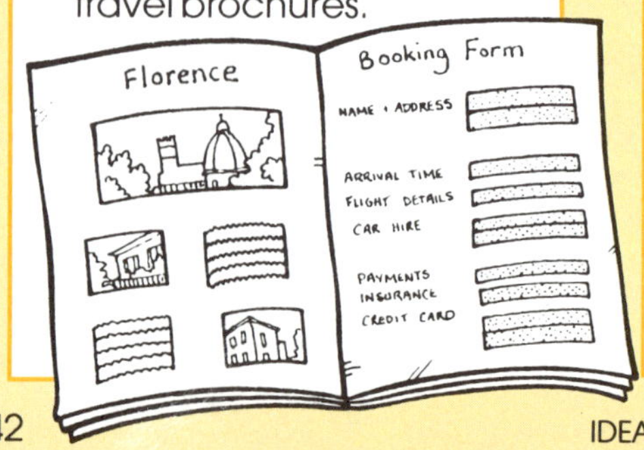


## Starting points

- Share with the children some of the junk mail received at school and ask them to collect some of the junk mail that arrives at their homes. Ask them about the sort of service this provides and what other sorts of print are delivered to their homes. The children could analyse the local free newspapers as described on page 40.
- Let them read the Ahlbergs' *The Jolly Postman* and share the mail in it with each other. They could look at how their collection of junk mail compares with that sent to the witch in the story.
- Make a collection of travel brochures featuring one particular country. More able children could use brochures that cover several different parts of the world. Identify how readers of travel brochures are helped to pick their holidays. Children who have visited a travel agent could describe how computers are used to find out if accommodation and flights are available.

## Extension activities

- The children could look for places to visit in their own area. Hotel and tourist information offices often provide leaflets covering a wide area.
- They could find references in local newspapers to the wider world, for example advertisements for holidays and twinned exchanges.
- The children could scan the *Yellow Pages* to find the names and numbers of local travel agents and taxi and coach firms that might take them to the airport.

 

# Sun and fun

Orlando temperatures

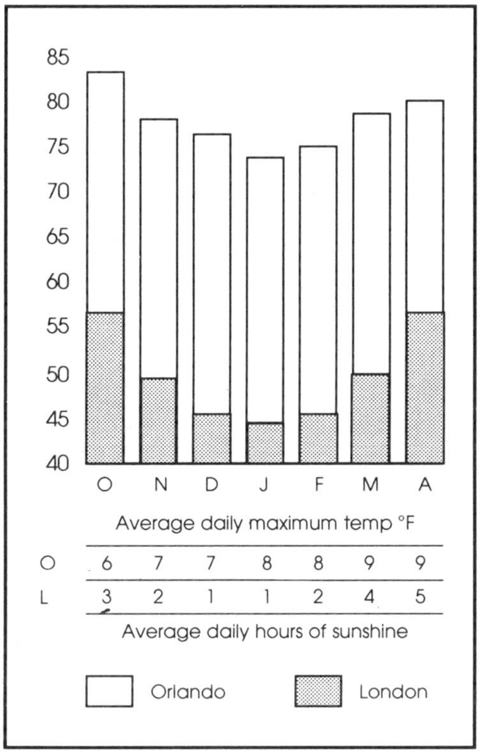


- What do 'O', 'N', 'D', 'J', 'F', 'M' and 'A' on the horizontal axis stand for?

- What does '°F' mean?

- In which month does London have the least average daily hours of sunshine?

- Which is the sunniest month in Orlando according to this table?

- Which is the warmest month?

Look at this hotel accommodation chart.

- What is the name of the hotel?

- How much would it cost for a room for four flying out on 21 December?

- How much would the same room cost flying out the next day?

- Does this include breakfast?

| **14 nights** | THE INTERNATIONAL | | |
|---|---|---|---|
| Board arrangements | Room only | | |
| Flights available | Fri, Sat | | |
| Number of Adults | 4 share | 3 share | 2 share |
| DEPARTURES ON OR BETWEEN | | | |
| 01 Nov–03 Nov | 349 | 363 | 405 |
| 04 Nov–17 Nov | 335 | 349 | 391 |
| 18 Nov–14 Dec | 315 | 329 | 371 |
| 15 Dec–21 Dec | 495 | 509 | 551 |
| 22 Dec–28 Dec | 569 | 583 | 625 |
| 29 Dec–04 Jan | 379 | 393 | 435 |
| 05 Jan–08 Feb | 315 | 329 | 371 |
| 09 Feb–15 Feb | 359 | 373 | 415 |
| 16 Feb–21 Mar | 345 | 359 | 401 |
| 22 Mar–28 Mar | 429 | 443 | 485 |
| 29 Mar–11 Apr | 545 | 559 | 601 |
| 12 Apr–20 Apr | 379 | 393 | 435 |
| **7 nts** SUBTRACT | 30 | 37 | 58 |
| **21 nts** ADD | 40 | 47 | 68 |

## Aims

- To raise awareness of print on some everyday products that are worn and used.

## Starting points

- Look at the print we wear, such as labels on clothes and footwear, writing on T-shirts and sweatshirts. Ask the children to record the sort of information it provides for us.
- List some of the structural print that can be found around the school, such as the name of the school, 'EXIT' and 'ENTRANCE' signs, rooms with printed signs and so on.
- See who can find the most print from the neighbourhood, such as street and shop signs, advertisements on billboards and buses, notices on poles and labels (including non-written symbols). Are there any signs that are in more than one language or in another script?

## Activities

- The activity sheet could be used as a home activity. The purpose is to demonstrate how much print there is in our everyday lives and how necessary it is.
- This can be extended to recording the information on a world map.
- Find labels which contain a different script and use other information on the labels to find out where these products come from.
- Find examples of labels that show that the manufacturer is concerned about how the product is brought to the consumer.

## Extension activities

- Find out where other products we eat originate from, for example turkeys, spaghetti, pizzas and tomatoes.
- Look in cookery books for some cheap and easy recipes that originate in other countries.

- The children could create a collage of fruit and vegetables from other countries and label the country (or countries) of origin. If available, collect supermarket recipes using these products.
- Use reference books to find out more about how food from other countries is produced and brought to this country. Teachers' resource books, such as Simon Fisher and David Hicks' *World Studies* and Miriam Steiner's *Learning from Experience* show how inequalities in trade can be explored with primary pupils.
- The children could make a collection of foreign coins and examine and compare the print on both sides of the coins.

# The world in a tin

- Collect the labels from some empty tins and food packets that come from other countries.
- Record the following information from the label. If the information is not available, leave a space.

| Name of product | Country of origin | Ingredients | Instruction for use | Consume by date |
|---|---|---|---|---|
| Tuna steak | Thailand | tuna, water, salt | | Dec '98 |
| | | | | |
| | | | | |
| | | | | |
| | | | | |
| | | | | |
| | | | | |
| | | | | |
| | | | | |
| | | | | |

- Choose one of the products and use reference books to find out more about the country it comes from and how it is produced.

## *Jokes, riddles and puns –* **Ideas page**

### Aims

- To appreciate that jokes, riddles, puns and limericks can be used as a means of developing linguistic understanding and confidence.
- To use research skills to find a collection of jokes.

### Starting points

- Ask the children to gather some 'knock, knock' jokes to be used as a reading resource.
- They could look at the pattern used to make the joke and try to make up their own.
- Make a collection of books that contains jokes, riddles, puns and limericks and let the children browse through them. These could include *The End* by Richard Stanley, *The Old Joke Book* by Janet and Allan Ahlberg, *Revolting Rhymes* by Roald Dahl and *Jokes, Jokes, Jokes* (Ladybird/Save the Children Fund).

### Extension activities

- Make a riddle chart or board with riddles and puns found and/or created by the children themselves.
- Ask them to read and use limericks as models for their own writing.

Rhyming words that need to be replaced could be highlighted.

- Look at and create cartoon riddle rhymes such as 'What did Miss Muffet see?'
  *Answer: a spider beside her.*
  'What do you call a cat who tells jokes?'
  *Answer: a witty kitty.*
- Make up and play with alliterative tongue twisters, for example 'Mad monsters munch many marshmallows.'

### Activities

- Let the children illustrate in a literal way a number of colloquialisms.

- They could use the joke book collection to make their own collection of subject-specific jokes such as elephant, school and monster jokes. For example:
  'Why does an elephant have wrinkled feet?'
  *Answer: to give the ants half a chance.*

 

# Sharing jokes

- *Use joke books to find four really funny jokes for this clown to tell.*

# Eight ways to help ...

There are hundreds of ideas in this book to enable you to develop and extend the photocopiable pages. Here are just eight ways to help you make the most of the Ideas Bank series.

**1**

Photocopy a page, paste it on to card and laminate/cover with sticky-backed plastic to use with groups. Children can write on the pages using water-based pens, which can be washed off.

**2**

Photocopy on to both sides of the paper. Put another useful activity on the back. Develop a simple filing system so others can find relevant sheets and do not duplicate them again.

**3**

Save the sheets – if the children do not have to cut them up as a part of the activity – and re-use. Label the sets and keep them safely in files.

**4**

Make the most of group work. Children working in small groups need only one sheet to discuss between them.

**5**

Put the sheets inside clear plastic wallets. The sheets are then easily stored in a binder and will last longer. Children's writing can again be wiped away.

**6**

Use as an ideas page for yourself. Discuss issues with the class and get the children to produce artwork and writing.

**7**

Make an overhead transparency of the page. You and your colleagues can then use the idea time and time again.

**8**

Ask yourself, 'Does every child in this class/group need to deal with/work through this photocopiable sheet?' If not, don't photocopy it!

 